About Parrots

To the One who created parrots
—*Genesis* 1:21

Published by
PEACHTREE PUBLISHERS
1700 Chattahoochee Avenue
Atlanta, Georgia 30318-2112
www.peachtree-online.com

Text © 2014 by Cathryn P. Sill
Illustrations © 2014 by John C. Sill

Illustrations created in watercolor on archival quality 100% rag watercolor paper;
text and titles typeset in Novarese from Adobe Systems

Printed and manufactured in March 2014 by Imago in Singapore

10 9 8 7 6 5 4 3 2 1
First Edition

Library of Congress Cataloging-in-Publication Data

Sill, Cathryn P., 1953- author.
  About parrots : a guide for children / Cathryn Sill, John Sill.
      pages cm
  Includes bibliographical references.
  ISBN 978-1-56145-795-3
  1. Parrots—Juvenile literature. 2. Parrots—Pictoral works. I. Sill, John, illustrator. II.
Title.
  QL696.P7S55 2014
  598.7'1—dc23
                          2013036723

About Parrots

A Guide for Children

Cathryn Sill

Illustrated by John Sill

Ω

PEACHTREE
ATLANTA

Parrots are birds with big heads and thick, curved bills.

They have sturdy legs and strong feet.
Each foot has two toes in front and two in back.

PLATE 2
Blue Lorikeet

Most parrots use their feet to climb
and swing from branches.

Parrots can bring food to their mouths with their feet.

PLATE 4
Blue-and-yellow Macaw

They eat seeds, nuts, fruits, leaves, flowers, and nectar.

Some parrots eat meat.

Parrots use their strong bills
and thick tongues to get food.

PLATE 7
Rainbow Lorikeet

Most parrots live in warm forests.
They can find plenty to eat there.

PLATE 8
Scarlet Macaw
(also shown: Mealy Amazon)

A few live in open areas or cooler places.

PLATE 9
Rosy-faced Lovebird

Some parrots are big. Others are small.

Many parrots live in noisy flocks.

They talk to each other with loud squawks, screams, or twitters.

PLATE 12
Thick-billed Parrot

Parrots have to be careful of birds of prey during the day.

Parrots roost in large groups at night. Sleeping together keeps them safe from snakes and mammals.

Most parrots have nest holes in trees.

PLATE 15
African Grey Parrot

Some parrots dig burrows for their nests.

PLATE 16
Burrowing Parrot
Hooded Parrot

Only one kind of parrot builds a stick nest away from holes and burrows.

It is important to protect parrots
and the places where they live.

Afterword

PLATE 1

There are more than 350 species of parrots. Wild parrots are native to all continents except Europe and Antarctica. Most of them live in the southern half of the world. Palm Cockatoos have an unusual way of using tools. With their foot, they grasp a stick or a nut and hit it against a hollow tree trunk to make a drumming sound. Palm Cockatoos live in New Guinea and other nearby islands, as well as in Cape York Peninsula, Australia.

PLATE 2

Parrots have zygodactyl feet, which means each foot has two toes facing forward and two toes facing backward. This foot structure helps them perform tasks differently from most birds, which have three toes forward and one back. Blue Lorikeets live on some Polynesian Islands. These small parrots have become extinct on some islands because rats and cats that were brought there by humans preyed on them. Illegal hunting for the pet trade has also caused problems for Blue Lorikeets.

PLATE 3

Parrots use their bills as well as their feet to climb. They also use their feet to grip perches, preen their feathers, and clean their bills. Parrots often hang from their feet while feeding. One group of parrots called "hanging parrots" sleeps hanging upside down. Blue-topped Hanging Parrots are small parrots that live in parts of Southeast Asia.

PLATE 4

Parrots are the only birds that can use their feet like hands to bring food up to their mouths. Other types of birds have to bend their heads down to eat food held in their claws. Blue-and-yellow Macaws eat a variety of nuts, fruits, and seeds. They are able to crack nuts easily with their powerful bills. Even though Blue-and-yellow Macaws are common in parts of Central and South America, their numbers are decreasing because of habitat loss and because so many of their nests have been raided for the pet trade.

PLATE 5

All parrots have hooked bills. The size and shape of the bills help determine the food parrots eat. Thick, heavy bills are used to crack tough nuts and fruits. Longer, thinner bills can be used to rake seeds from fruits. Dusky-billed Parrotlets eat seeds from cecropia trees. They live in the Amazon River basin and other parts of northern South America.

PLATE 6

Several kinds of parrots eat insect larvae, insects, and other small invertebrates, as well as plant parts. Keas are omnivores whose food includes grubs, insects, and land snails along with flowers, berries, roots, leaves, and stems. They also eat carrion and sometimes search for food on trash dumps. Keas live in the mountains of South Island, New Zealand. They are one of the few types of parrots that live in colder climates. For years, Keas were killed because farmers believed they attacked and ate sheep.

PLATE 7

The top part of a parrot's bill curves down over the bottom part. This forms a strong tool that helps the parrot eat as well as climb and dig nest holes. Parrots' tongues are thick and muscular. They use their tongues to explore their surroundings and find food. Some parrots such as the Rainbow Lorikeet have a brush-like tip on their tongue that gathers nectar and pollen from flowers. Rainbow Lorikeets live in parts of Indonesia, New Guinea, and Australia.

PLATE 8

While many kinds of parrots live in tropical rainforests, some are also found in temperate forests. Scarlet Macaws live in tropical forests, often close to rivers. They sometimes join other kinds of parrots at clay licks. They eat the clay to get salt. Eating soil from clay licks also protects parrots from poisons found in some seeds. Scarlet Macaws live in Central and South America.

PLATE 9

Some kinds of parrots live in places without many trees. A few of them live high in mountains where the weather is cooler. Others live in deserts. Rosy-faced Lovebirds live in dry areas of southwestern Africa. They live near rivers or other sources of water.

PLATE 10

Hyacinth Macaws are the longest parrots. They are 40 inches (100 cm) long. Hyacinth Macaws have very large bills that are strong enough to crack tough palm nuts. They are endangered because of habitat loss and illegal trapping for the pet trade. They live in parts of eastern and central South America. Buff-faced Pygmy Parrots are the smallest parrots. They are less than 4 inches (8 cm) long. Buff-faced Pygmy Parrots eat lichen, bark funguses, insects, small seeds, and fruit. They live in New Guinea.

PLATE 11

Parrot flocks are often loud. Their squawks, shrieks, and twitters can be heard from some distance away. Most parrots are sociable and spend time together. They stay in groups as they cuddle, feed, and roost. Galahs are cockatoos that live in open country in Australia. They often form flocks of several hundred birds.

PLATE 12

In the forest it is often easier to hear green-colored parrots than it is to see them. But as they fly overhead, the noisy flocks are hard to miss. The calls of Thick-billed Parrots can be heard up to 1 mile (1.6 km) away. Thick-billed Parrots live in the mountains of northern Mexico. They do not mind cold weather. Thick-billed Parrots used to live in the southwestern United States. They no longer live there and are endangered in Mexico because the pine forests where they live are being cut down.

PLATE 13
Parrots stay alert and are hard for predators to catch during the day. Living together in flocks helps keep them safe from raptors (birds of prey). Cobalt-winged Parakeets live in tropical forests in northwestern parts of South America.

PLATE 14
Mammals and snakes have a hard time catching flying parrots, but they can more easily sneak up on resting birds. When parrots are at rest, it is safer for them to gather together in large groups. If danger is near, parrots make lots of noise to warn the rest of the flock. Eclectus Parrots roost in groups of up to eighty birds. The colors of the males and females are so different that people used to believe they were two separate species. They live on some islands in Indonesia and in northeastern Australia.

PLATE 15
Nest holes help protect baby parrots from predators and weather. Most parrots do not make their own tree holes. They use holes made by other birds such as woodpeckers, or holes that are already in the tree. Parrots may use their bills to make the hole larger. A few kinds of parrots dig holes in trees that have soft wood. The nest holes of African Grey Parrots are usually high in a tree. African Grey Parrots live in central Africa.

PLATE 16

Parrots that dig burrows use termite mounds, cliffs, or banks for their nests. Most parrots that nest in termite mounds use those located in trees. Some kinds of parrots, such as Hooded Parrots, make their burrows in termite mounds that are on the ground. Termites can still be living in the mounds. Hooded Parrots live in Australia. Burrowing Parrots dig burrows for nests in sandstone and limestone cliffs near rivers and the ocean. They live in dry open country in southern South America.

PLATE 17

Some types of parrots use sticks or grass to build nests inside holes. If they cannot find a hole in a tree, they have to build nests of sticks in other places. Monk Parakeets build large nests that may have several rooms for different families. The nest has separate entrances for each pair. Monk Parakeets are native to southeastern South America but have been introduced to many places in North America and Europe.

PLATE 18

About one third of all species of parrots are endangered or threatened. Some are in trouble because their habitats are being destroyed. Others have problems because people capture the adults or take the babies from their nests to sell as pets. It is now illegal to sell wild parrots for the pet trade. Kakapos are flightless parrots that live on the ground. They have nearly become extinct because of predators such as cats and rats that were introduced by humans. Kakapos live in New Zealand.

GLOSSARY

Carrion—dead and decaying flesh

Endangered—threatened with becoming extinct (no longer existing)

Habitat—the place where animals and plants live and grow

Invertebrate—an animal that does not have a backbone, such as an insect or a worm

Native—an animal or plant that lives naturally in a place

Omnivore—an animal that eats both meat and plants

Predator—an animal that lives by hunting and eating other animals

Preen—to straighten or clean feathers

Roost—to rest or sleep

Species—a group of animals or plants that are alike in many ways

Temperate—not very hot and not very cold

SUGGESTIONS FOR FURTHER READING

BOOKS

A RAINBOW OF PARROTS by Vicki León (London Town Press)

PARROTS (NATURE'S CHILDREN) by Ruth Bjorklund (Children's Press)

PARROTS AROUND THE WORLD by Mark J. Rauzon

WEBSITES

www.a-z-animals.com/animals/parrot

http://animals.nationalgeographic.com/animals/birds/parrot

RESOURCES ESPECIALLY HELPFUL IN DEVELOPING THIS BOOK

HANDBOOK OF THE BIRDS OF THE WORLD: Vol. 4, Edited by Josep del Hoyo, Andrew Elliott, Jordi Sargatal, and Jürgen H. Haffer (Lynx Edicions, Barcelona)

PARROTS: THE ANIMAL ANSWER GUIDE by Matt Cameron (The Johns Hopkins University Press)

PARROTS OF THE WORLD: AN IDENTIFICATION GUIDE by Joseph M. Forshaw (Princeton University Press)

ABOUT... SERIES

ISBN 978-1-56145-234-7 HC
ISBN 978-1-56145-312-2 PB

ISBN 978-1-56145-038-1 HC
ISBN 978-1-56145-364-1 PB

ISBN 978-1-56145-688-8 HC
ISBN 978-1-56145-699-4 PB

ISBN 978-1-56145-301-6 HC
ISBN 978-1-56145-405-1 PB

ISBN 978-1-56145-256-9 HC
ISBN 978-1-56145-335-1 PB

ISBN 978-1-56145-588-1 HC

ISBN 978-1-56145-207-1 HC
ISBN 978-1-56145-232-3 PB

About Mammals

ISBN 978-1-56145-757-1 HC
ISBN 978-1-56145-758-8 PB

ISBN 978-1-56145-358-0 HC
ISBN 978-1-56145-407-5 PB

ISBN 978-1-56145-331-3 HC
ISBN 978-1-56145-406-8 PB

About Parrots

ISBN 978-1-56145-795-3 HC

About Penguins

ISBN 978-1-56145-743-4 HC
ISBN 978-1-56145-741-0 PB

ISBN 978-1-56145-536-2 HC
ISBN 978-1-56145-811-0 PB

About Reptiles

ISBN 978-1-56145-183-8 HC
ISBN 978-1-56145-233-0 PB

ISBN 978-1-56145-454-9 HC

ALSO AVAILABLE IN BILINGUAL EDITION

- About Birds / Sobre los pájaros
  ISBN 978-1-56145-783-0 PB
- About Mammals / Sobre los mamíferos
  ISBN 978-1-56145-800-4 PB

ABOUT HABITATS SERIES

ISBN 978-1-56145-641-3 HC
ISBN 978-1-56145-636-9 PB

ISBN 978-1-56145-734-2 HC

ISBN 978-1-56145-559-1 HC

ISBN 978-1-56145-469-3 HC
ISBN 978-1-56145-731-1 PB

ISBN 978-1-56145-618-5 HC

ISBN 978-1-56145-432-7 HC
ISBN 978-1-56145-689-5 PB

THE SILLS

Cathryn Sill, a former elementary school teacher, is the author of the acclaimed ABOUT... series and ABOUT HABITATS series. With her husband John and her brother-in-law Ben Sill, she coauthored the popular bird-guide parodies, A FIELD GUIDE TO LITTLE-KNOWN AND SELDOM-SEEN BIRDS OF NORTH AMERICA, ANOTHER FIELD GUIDE TO LITTLE-KNOWN AND SELDOM-SEEN BIRDS OF NORTH AMERICA, and BEYOND BIRDWATCHING.

John Sill is a prize-winning and widely published wildlife artist who illustrated the ABOUT... series and ABOUT HABITATS series, and illustrated and coauthored the FIELD GUIDES and BEYOND BIRDWATCHING. A native of North Carolina, he holds a B.S. in Wildlife Biology from North Carolina State University.

The Sills live in Franklin, North Carolina.